Twenty Days
on Route 20

Michael Czarnecki

FootHills Publishing

ACKNOWLEDGEMENTS

I would like to thank the following individuals and businesses for their help in making the journey possible:

Rhonda Morton
Michael Gossie
Roger Neuhaus
Mary E. Seiler
Randy and Sally Cartwright
David and Dorrie Hipschman
Joseph and Ellen Kinnebrew
Gary Richardson and Diane Ronayne
Jennifer Gilden
KC's Corner Restaurant & Motel, East Springfield, NY
Canfield Hotel, Dubuque, IA
The Westerner Motel, Chadron, NE
Prairie View Campground, Lusk, WY
Pawnee Hotel, Cody, WY
Blue Haven Motel, Gardiner, MT
Bontemps Motel, Burns, OR
Conklin's Guest House, Sisters, OR
The LEADER, Corning, NY
The Freeport Journal, IL
The Auburn Citizen, NY

Portions of this book first appeared in The LEADER newspaper in Corning, NY in somewhat different form.

Cover photo by Michael Czarnecki
US 20 in the Sandhills of Nebraska.

ISBN: 0-941053-01-6

4th Printing April 2014

FootHills Publishing
PO Box 68
Kanona, NY 14856
www.foothillspublishing.com

*This book is
dedicated to:*

Matsuo Basho
Saigyo
David Grayson
Carolyn
Cassandra
Grayson
Chapin
Rhonda

and my old beat
1983 Honda Civic Wagon

Day 1

One travels because one must. Wanderlust, once felt, will always remain a part of one's self. Travel is not only for carefree, adventurous youth. Maybe, because of the responsibilities of growing older, the desire is held in abeyance for some time when we enter middle adulthood. It can be ignored for only so long before either the road is ventured onto again or one's dreams fade and life becomes a series of chores, any thoughts of the freedom of the road repressed - such thoughts too threatening, too subversive of the stable life we have settled into.

September twentieth. I said good-bye to Carolyn and my children, Cassandra, Grayson, Chapin and left home about 9:00 PM, heading east to go west. Friends waved good-bye as I drove off in the dark, not to return for nearly a month.

> some sadness leaving
> long road to distant places
> summer at an end

Driving through the night toward Boston on highways very familiar to me. All road adventures should start out in the dark night, driving toward some distant destination and the dawn. These expressways, NY 17, I-88, I-90, were very familiar, but this evening they seemed different. I had always driven these roads because they took me to some temporary final destination - the Adirondack mountains, Vermont, Acadia National Park. Got me to where I was going. This time, these familiar interstates were taking me to a place, but only so I could start the real road adventure. These were roads to get me to THE ROAD. The preliminaries, opening act, the warm-up exercise.

How the mind wanders, especially alone on a night highway with few other cars around, dark hills shadowing the horizon. How many times I've traveled this road over the last few years! Daytime, nighttime. Albany, Boston, Maine. It all feels like new territory now. In reality it is always new territory. We are forever and always a different person than who we were. Those previous trips up the Susquehanna Valley were taken by someone different than the person driving this old, beat Honda now. These dark hills are different than they've ever been. It's all new, all different each and every day. It is not just because this is the start of a grand adventure that I feel as if these hills are different tonight. They are as they've never been. I am as I've never been.

Twenty-five years ago, after a month of camping and backpacking in the Adirondacks, Green and White Mountains of New England, the rocky granite coast of Maine at Acadia, I found my way by thumb into downtown Boston. There I became bummed out because of that cold indifference to strangers that is so much a part of city life. Out on country roads, camped in campgrounds, hiking on mountain trails, people were friendly, curious, engaging. In the city it was totally the opposite. No words of greeting, no meeting eyes. The only people who spoke with me – a wino offering me a swig from his brown-bagged bottle of cheap wine and a cop who told me to get off the grass I was sitting on in the public garden.

At this point I just wanted to get out of the city before dark. As I walked and thumbed away from downtown another hitchhiker was standing along the side of Commonwealth with her thumb out. I intended to just walk by, start hitchhiking beyond – there is a hitchhiking courtesy that says you don't step in front of someone who was there ahead of you. Besides, I was now feeling like the other city denizens I had been experiencing – I didn't feel like looking at or talking to anyone else either – I just wanted to get out!

To say I was surprised to hear a "Hi!" as I walked by would be a huge understatement. I had given up on the city. When one stops wanting, desiring, stops trying...

We talked, hitched together. I stayed, we traveled to the Cape, made love (first time for each of us) and shared parts of the next two years of our lives. Terry. Third floor Beacon Street, address long ago forgotten.

In Boston, morning rush hour, searching for US 20, I found myself on Beacon Street. An old WPA travel guide to Massachusetts mentioned Route 20 traversing down Beacon. No signs. I parked, and as I walked I glanced up at the row houses looking for a familiar sign, an entranceway having once walked through arm in arm, laughter on our faces.

> seeking memories
> lost in haze of distant years
> dried leaf tumbles by

Row houses with similar steps leading up to the front door. A quarter of a century ago. I could still hear the laughter, could not pinpoint the house.

I asked numerous people about the whereabouts of Route 20 – no one knew, not even cab drivers! I received many directions to 20 in the suburbs – Cambridge, Brookline, Newton - but no hints for somewhere in Boston. So I drove out Beacon hoping for a beginning.

> finally a sign
> hanging askew on a pole
> now I can start west

Commonwealth Avenue just west of Beacon Street. US 20 no longer entered the city itself. Now the journey can begin!

I might have saved time if I had researched US 20 in other than that WPA Guidebook from a half century ago... But then I would not have walked down Beacon Street, would not have heard that laughter from so long ago.

I asked a young woman walking by if she would take a few photos of me standing under the sign. She did, but when I explained my journey and asked if she'd like me to send her a picture she replied, "Noooo thanks" and walked hurriedly away. Ah, cities!

Road curvy, windy, bumpy (under re-construction in places) through Brookline, Watertown, Waltham. Crossing the Charles River I recalled that first night with Terry in Boston: a free New York Rock and Roll Ensemble concert along river, warm summer night and 50,000 people spread out on green grass smoking pot, drinking wine, dancing. I remember nothing of the music. We talked, sipped Mateus from the bottle, explored getting to know each other. Those long ago carefree encounters. How often do we explore paths like that nowadays?

Waltham. Wilson's Diner. Mid-40's bus-like eatery. The long night drive, searching for the past, searching for a start and not a bite to eat. This first meal on the journey, fitting to be in one of the old road diners that hark back to the heyday of the auto era. Greek sandwiches and usual other fare. Though lunchtime, I order hash browns and eggs - breakfast served all day.

Talked with Gordon, sitting in the booth next to me, about folk and country music. He is president of the New England Country Music Historical Society. Doesn't play himself but thoroughly enjoys hearing others perform traditional music. Interest in creativity is everywhere!

In the old traveling days the backpack, sleeping bag and tent tied to the frame, would be standing near the door or on the seat opposite me, an obvious sign that I was a traveler on the road. Now I carry no such calling card, just a journal and map, all else left in the car. Just another customer eating his mid-day breakfast.

Feels good to be on the road. Moving, experiencing along the way, not just hurrying along to get somewhere else. The experience of the journey itself. Here and now, being in the moment, not looking ahead to where I'm headed. Being as much as possible in the present.

Finally the road opening up, leaving suburban, greater Boston area behind. Farmland, fields, small towns. This rural route the quintessential cross-country American experience. It is not the populated cities that capture my imagination when thinking of this vast country, but the fields, farms, hills, valleys, rivers, lakes, mountains, deserts. People are an important part, but in large cities they seem so distant, so far away. Give me small towns and small cities separated by open spaces of earth and sky.

Route 20 between Worcester and Springfield traverses apple country. Orchards, or orchard signs, are never far away. A sign for Charlton Orchards, just west of Auburn, drew me in. A quarter mile oak-lined lane leads up to the orchards and store. As I pull up a busload of young schoolchildren drives away. I never took a field trip to an apple orchard when I was a young student in Buffalo!

What else could be more refreshing on the doorstep of autumn than a nice cool drink of fresh pressed cider? I buy a half gallon and drink half of that before even getting back onto 20! Talk about the essence of the northeast, the flavor of autumn! The only other taste that can compete with apple cider, as far as representing a season and a region, is possibly that of ripe cranberries on a northern November day scooped up out of the water while paddling a canoe on a creek in downeast Maine. Cranberries, eaten fresh from the water, have that raw bitter taste of a northern November day. Fresh pressed apple cider has the exact flavor of a northeastern hill country autumn day in every sip.

Palmer, Massachusetts. A Salvation Army store drew my attention. Nothing jumped out at me to purchase, but then I noticed the Palmer Public Library so stopped to see if I could plug in the computer to write the first of the daily columns from the journey that were being published in The Leader, back home in Steuben County, NY. While writing, the director came up to me and we talked about the journey. Before leaving he gave me a Palmer Library T-shirt and we talked of coming back to give a reading someday.

From there, westward, as the end of the first day of the journey was coming on. The Berkshires. Westfield River, rock outcroppings, winding road through a narrow valley. Needing to move on, I thought this would be a great place to explore sometime in the future. Then Robert Frost's "Stopping By Woods On a Snowy Evening" and "The Road Not Taken" came into mind. New England countryside. Mountains, valleys, places drawing my attention and yet, "miles to go before I sleep," and "I doubted if I should ever come back." Already realizing that on this journey I will mostly be passing through, staying a very short while in a very few places between the Atlantic and the Pacific.

So, my first night out I slept in the Honda at a rest area not far from the New York State border. I cleared out the back, folded down the back seats, unrolled the sleeping bag, curled up under the light of a first quarter moon shining above a mountain to the south. I slept well. A night reminiscent of other long ago nights, sleeping bag and tarp off the side of the road, in the woods, under a bridge, in the tall grass on an embankment above an expressway. The vagabond, no fixed address, no bed to sleep in, wandering the roads of America, not sure what each new day would bring.

Day 2

Next morning, after a short walk in the woods up the hill from the car, I headed back out on 20 and just around the bend came to a vista off to the west that I just had to stop for.

> green hills rise up from
> fog covering valley floor
> cars just speeding by

As I stood taking in the view one other car pulled up, the driver staying inside, soaking up the distant fog and hilltop laden vista. Bill, who lives just down the road in Pittsfield, says he stops here often. Lebanon Valley Lookout he tells me. "I'll be here looking at the view and the cars just keep passing by and nobody stops, nobody looks." Bill talked of bike trips he had been on. Another traveler, another spirit knowing the value of capturing those fleeting moments of wonder that punctuate our short, often sorrowful existence.

Continuing down into Lebanon Valley, Massachusetts behind, the long stretch of New York State and familiar territory ahead, I started feeling like I was settling into the journey. Adjusting to the road, the movement, the going, going, going that is the one constant of all true travelers. I crossed a state boundary, a fictional line that has no bearing to geography, hills poking up from dense valley covering fog. I know the abstractness of that line yet still felt as though I passed one marker on the long road west. But more than that, I was beginning once again to feel the pleasure, the joy of the moving itself.

Bill told me of the Lark Street Festival that would be going on today in Albany. 20 goes right by Lark Street (I'm somewhat familiar with the city) so I thought I'd stop to check it out. Lark Street was closed off for maybe six blocks and arts and crafts people were setting up booths. Early morning, the festival wasn't open yet, but I browsed, bought a few old albums and some books from a table operated by an AIDS/HIV support group.

While looking at the records I asked someone next to me how far route 20 goes to the west. He replied, "Schenectedy, I think." I didn't let on that I knew it went much, much further. Actually, 20 doesn't even go through Schenectedy at all!

Another breakfast at a diner. This time a step-down-off-the-street place on one of the festival blocks: "Albany Coffee Shop." Sam, the owner, maybe 60 or so, balding, glasses, asked if I was one of the "artists from out there?" I told him no, spoke of the trip, the book. "So you're writing a book. Good, good!"

A long narrow space, counter seats, no tables and chairs, kitchen in back. Old Kelvinator Ice Cream Freezer, wooden desk, brass and wooden register, old heavy black-based fan for warmer days, ceramic figurines — a woman with long dress, umbrella, flowers and a Labatt's Pilsener Swiss Alp lederhosen wearing chap. A step back in time.

```
┌─────────────────────────────────────────────┐
│                   SPECIAL                     │
│  Sausage on Hard Roll w/peppers and onions 2.50 │
└─────────────────────────────────────────────┘
```

Sounds like a haiku almost!

A good hearty breakfast of homefries, eggs over easy, coffee, then back up the stairs, onto the street, out on the road.

Called, then visited with, an old friend from the traveling days I haven't seen for eleven years. Back in 1972 Bob was inspired to quit his job (which he didn't like anyway) because of all the hitchhiking I had been doing. He then spent four and a half years away from the states, living in Australia, journeying around the world. Now, at 51, he feels those were the happiest years of his life. There's still dreams - a sailboat in the Caribbean, maybe returning to Australia - but there's also concerns about getting in enough years of work for decent retirement benefits, health insurance. Maybe going back to Australia, but. . .

I drive away from his house back toward US 20, think of my being on the road again, think of my Uncle Ed, one of my closest relatives. He could have retired early, at 52 or so, but decided to work a few more years at the steel mill to get better benefits. One night, about a year later, he was sitting in the living room making plans with a longtime friend for camping, fishing, hunting the following year - he had 13 weeks of vacation coming. Uncle Ed never woke up again. Over twenty years ago now. The steel mill long gone. What might he have done if. . .

For a long time now I have viewed life as if death were hanging over my left shoulder. Any moment I might feel the pressure of the hand weigh down on me, guide me out of this present world. That vision has certainly affected many of the decisions I have made in my life.

The Hudson River flows through Albany. I wanted to spend a little time along it but the area where 20 crosses is highway and industrial and not very inviting. Then I drove by Corning Preserve, a riverside greenway along the west bank. Stopping, I discovered The River Front Bar and Grill anchored along side of the Preserve. An old barge brought here from Rhode Island and renovated to become a floating restaurant. It just opened a few weeks ago but already seems to be a popular place.

The owner let me bring the computer aboard. He put a table near an outlet and I sat on the upper deck writing on my old Mac Classic II. A woman at a nearby table exclaimed, "I thought I had the oldest computer around!"

Cormorants and gulls fly by, pleasure boats ply the water and a light breeze blows from the river. The barge rocks gently in the current, sun shines warm on my face. I finish one brew and a bowl of French Onion soup, then linger through a second beer. When ready to leave, Brubeck comes on the speakers, "Take Five." I decide to linger a little longer.

resting on Hudson
four-decades-old jazz holds me
summer's last full day

20 is a great driving road through New York. Even in Albany traffic flows along smoothly without a whole lot of stops. West of the city

the road gets back out into rural country, rolling hills and small towns spaced just the right distance apart. Great vistas every now and then of distant Adirondack mountains to the north. Antique shops and farms, rock outcroppings along the side of the road, big old farmhouses with big old maple trees growing next to them.

When traveling, food becomes of prime interest. Where will I eat tonight? What about this morning's breakfast? When one isn't out vagabonding there is the kitchen cupboard, cookstove, family meal. On the road, alone, it's diners, restaurants, easy eating food in the car.

In the dark night, US 20, East Springfield, upstate New York, the lights of KC's Corner Restaurant & Motel called out for me to stop, relax, grab a bite to eat. Open for all three meals, all year. A pleasure to sit down in a booth with book, journal and coffee. Haddock, mashed potatoes, corn, 2" thick slice of homemade bread — $7.50. A not too populated small town, rural country area yet the restaurant was doing a good business, even this late (8:00 pm) Saturday night.

As I sat eating my meal I began considering where I would sleep for the night. KC's Corner Restaurant & Motel – hmmm! This was a low budget journey and I couldn't be spending much money on places to sleep. The second night out was too early to succumb to the temptation of a soft, comfortable bed in a motel. Then one of those sudden inspirations came to me – why not barter for a room!

I hesitatingly walked up to the owner of KC's and explained my journey to him. I mentioned that I would be writing a book and that if he let me use a room for the night I would acknowledge KC's on the acknowledgement page and then give him enough books to cover the cost of the room. To my surprise he immediately accepted the offer! This spontaneous idea changed the whole character of the rest of the trip.

I had never done this before, barter writings for lodgings. Felt a little bit like Vachel Lindsay, the early 20th Century poet from Springfield, Illinois. I remember reading his work as a junior in high school and being excited to learn that he went on walking

14

trips, exchanging rhymes for room and board. Poetry had real world value! So now, 30 years later, here I was in a comfortable room because of someone's willingness to accept written words for payment. Mr. Kerr, if only you could know how as a teacher you changed my life!

Had a good talk with the owner about local history, Route 20 and how more people seem to be driving the road now than a decade or so ago. Also told me that up the road a little way I'd pass one of the oldest toll houses still around from the old days when 20 was known as Turnpike Road. It's just an old abandoned house, last used by an antique dealer for storage. In the 19th century this was a privately maintained thoroughfare and tolls were collected at various locations for the privilege of using the road.

After our talk I unpacked what I needed from the car, set up the old Mac in the room, wrote a little and then had a comfortable sleep that was so much better than the night before in the back of the Honda.

Day 3

After a great night's rest I stepped outside, heading to the restaurant for breakfast.

> first day of autumn
> flock of geese call overhead
> they too, moving on

An omen? First day of my favorite season, flock of geese greeting me as I step out into the morning air.

Then, after breakfast, checking the car's oil and water, I got talking with a couple from Germany who also stayed at the motel. They have been traveling around the northeast: Boston, NYC, Pennsylvania, Toronto, Niagara Falls. A meteorologist in Germany, he just had an interview for a position with a national weather forecasting company in Pennsylvania. They're hoping to be able to come over to the states to work and live for a few years. When I told them of my journey, the first thing he said was "like Route 66." Everyone has heard about Route 66, almost no one knows very much about 20! This was the first of many times I would hear Route 66 brought up in relation to my journey on US 20.

The old tollhouse was easy to spot. A "For Sale" sign was posted on the front and inside a few scattered bottles and things. The tollhouse stood on a knoll in the road, another side road went off perpendicular to the south. I wondered how long ago the last toll was collected at this spot.

> weathered old tollhouse
> people speed by, pay no mind
> take from me this poem

A few miles down the road I realized I should have left a copy of this haiku tacked to the front door of the tollhouse. Maybe when I pass this way again.

US 20 is an historic thoroughfare. Through Massachusetts and New York it was one of the main roads heading out toward the western wilderness. How many folks traveled it with dreams of new beginnings somewhere west? That west was always changing, too. Western New York, Ohio, the plains, the far northwest. I dream of what lies ahead on my journey, western landscapes I've never seen. Yet, when done traveling, I'll return home to the hills of the Finger Lakes. Those settlers who ventured west on the turnpike were dreaming of making a home for themselves in the wide open spaces somewhere beyond the horizon. They were the real travelers. How can I even imagine I'm one in my 83 Honda Wagon and a comfortable home to return to?

Rolling hill country upstate New York Route 20. Antiques, dairy farms, apple orchards. Light rain begins to fall, then occasional heavy downpours that make it hard to see through the windshield. Uphill, downhill. Light rain, heavy rain. Summer, autumn. Familiar ground, new ground.

A short stop at Bouckville, antique center of Route 20. At a pavilion full of dealers I stop at one stall featuring postcards and ask if they have any of Route 20. We search through "Roadside" grouping and nothing. Again, Route 66, no 20!

Cazenovia. Small village of shops, Victorian houses, adjacent rolling hills. Small lake of the same name just west of the village.

> stillness of water
> quiet Cazenovia
> rest here a minute

A few canoers in parking area at south end of lake where 20 skirts by. Colorful rain slickers, hats, coming in off the water. A wet day for canoeing. I sit in the car instead of venturing out in the light misty rain.

> granite blocks on shore
> framed by white blooming asters
> intermittent rain

Beyond Lafayette numerous signs for Beak & Skiff Apple Orchards. I turn off 20 where the sign points south and drive a half mile to reach the orchards. Sunday afternoon, pouring rain in the rolling rural hills of New York and the parking lot is full of cars! I park as rain comes down in buckets. On the porch of the store stand throngs of people. What a hopping, busy place! Not at all like the much smaller orchard I stopped at in Massachusetts.

I ran out of the car and squeezed onto the porch. Inside, people milling around watching cider being pressed, browsing shelves full of honey, cheese, apple bread, pickled onions, sweatshirts, gift packs to be sent through the mail, and even apples! One of the managers told me that this wasn't a very busy day! What was it like on a busy day, I wondered. The cider was a wonderful treat.

When leaving Beak & Skiff I saw a sign on the side road, "Tony's Garlic" with an arrow pointing away from 20. I turned that way, knowing Carolyn wanted to reestablish a garlic bed this fall with some new garlic. I found Tony in his garage amidst bunches of hanging garlic and strings of various kinds of hot peppers. He's been growing garlic for 10 years. I bought a bunch for planting and when I was leaving he advised, "Make sure you put them the first or second weekend of October. And make sure you break off the seed heads next June."

Skaneateles Lake. The north end comes right up to the village. Choppy water, not calm like Cazenovia. The first of the Finger Lakes seen from 20.

> lowering gray clouds
> hills obscured, lake water dark
> couple walks on shore

Entered Auburn on a beautiful street with a grassy, tree filled mall down the middle then exited on a divided highway devoid of any connection with the city! Auburn is the first city on 20 since Albany, some 150 or so miles away. The stretch of Route 20 between those two cities is simply wonderful. Rolling hills, picturesque villages, farms and scenic views. A truly enjoyable drive.

Beyond Auburn the hills disappear for the most part and the land
swells in little rises and dips. Not as pleasing to the eye as east of
Auburn, but still pleasant landscape to travel through.
I decided to detour through Montezuma Wildlife Refuge. The
entrance to the 3.5 mile drive-through is right along 20. Managed
marsh land, Interstate 90 just to the north.

> two great blue herons
> glide over car, call "gawk, gawk"
> rain has stopped falling

Seneca Falls, the birthplace of the Women's Movement. The first
women's convention held here. Susan B. Anthony one of the main
forces behind the movement. A National Women's Rights Museum
located in the center of the village.

The long sweep of Seneca Lake, deepest – 630', and second longest
- 38 miles, of the 11 Finger Lakes, as 20 passes around the edge of
Geneva. Canandaigua: hardly any experience of village, lake. New
by-pass road avoids both. I should have stopped, should have . . .

Then detour off 20 to home, a night with family. 12th wedding
anniversary. An interlude from the road.

Day 4

In morning, back up to 20, then west. In rear view mirror gray clouds trailing off in the distance. Ahead, blue sky, sunshine and old hometown of Buffalo. Today I pass beyond the known route, head west from the city where I was raised, the city where I always took off to the east in the old days of traveling. A turning point.

How many times those many years ago did I leave Buffalo with pack and thumb, heading east? Everyone seemed to head west in those days - Colorado, San Francisco, Rocky Mountains, Pacific Ocean. For me - New England, Maritimes, Acadia shore, Green and White Mountains, Adirondacks. Always a direction away from the crowd. Now, I finally move west, move opposite my path of 25 years ago.

20 traverses around the edge of Buffalo, never entering the city. In one of the suburbs I met with an old friend and painter for breakfast. Our friendship goes back to those long ago traveling days, though we've never traveled together. If I didn't feel the need to make this cross country journey alone, he would be the perfect companion. Mellow, easygoing, seeing with an artist's eye.

One of the most memorable hikes I've ever taken was with him, years ago, up Champlain Mountain in Acadia National Park. We were up top on the long ridge when fog blew in from the ocean making it impossible to see very far. We settled down on some rocks, talked, took in the view, waited till fog lifted, vision became clear once again. Two friends sitting on hard granite, enveloped in soft misty vapors, ocean far down below, dust of the world distant. Not often do we find ourselves in such surroundings. I don't remember what words were spoken. We may have been mostly silent. Sometimes that is preferable. Yet, that experience is etched forever in my consciousness.

A good breakfast, good talk and then outside the restaurant a young oriental woman walked up to us selling wind chimes. She's from Taiwan and travels around with other young people raising money for the World Carp Academy, based in Boulder. We have a pleasant talk about her life, creativity, spirituality. I ask her name in Chinese: Yun-Ju. She writes her name for me in Chinese characters. We part pleasantly, though neither of us bought a wind chime. A more pleasant encounter than I ever had with Jesus freaks or Hare Krishnas in the old days.

another goodbye
leaving birth city behind
first full day of fall

I drive away, south then west around the city. Memories of friends and lovers flood back from those long ago days - Margaret, Cindy, Mike, Joe, Harry, Tony, Sandy, Lorna, Diane, Donna, Tom. Another lifetime, another space, another person. How different am I, really? The journey. Outward - twenty days on Route 20. Inward - a lifetime past, a lifetime future.

A change in geography. From just west of Boston to near Buffalo, 20 encounters continuous hills, mountains, rivers, the road often seeming to run counter to the natural landscape. Crossing, always crossing, the flow of the terrain. Now, south and west of Buffalo, in the Lake Erie plain, the road travels with the contour of the land. To the south and east a ridge parallels the lake, a mile or so away. The lake itself is always a few miles off to the west and north, hardly ever in view. A brief distant glimmer. A road between the hills and the lake, never coming too close to either, keeping each an arm's length away.

Filled up on gas at Native Pride Indian Trading Post on the Cattaraugus Reservation. $1.07/gallon. US 20 cuts through Seneca territory here and the Senecas sell gas and cigarettes much cheaper than elsewhere because of the absence of federal and state taxes. A political/legal controversy brews over the revenue New York State feels it's losing because of the Seneca's insistence of being a sovereign nation.

I drive away from the reservation (that word itself seems so insulting) having traveled about 500 miles on my journey and am now starting to feel how this land is all connected, all a part of something much larger, much more important than artificial

political lines drawn on maps and legalized in some grandiose governmental building in some far away center of "power."
Short stop in Fredonia at White Pine Press. An upstairs office space behind the square in this small, Lake Erie plains village. So much of poetic worth and inspiration comes forth from this small insignificant space.

Outside, sitting in the square, a bee buzzes around me, lands on my bare arm, flies an inch or two from my face. No bother. No threat, he or I.

Grape country! Miles and miles of vineyards, scattered here and there and then at times continuous, along this near Lake Erie stretch of road. So different than the rolling hills, woodlands, dairy farm terrain through western Massachusetts and New York east of Buffalo.

Crossing that imaginary border again. This time the NY-Penn line. The roadway is changed, now divided, a different type of pavement, but landscape has stayed the same.

The road through Erie is not very interesting. Miles of rundown cityscape with nothing appealing to the senses. The only exception - adults and children planting flowers on the grounds of a school. A bit of hope in an otherwise dreary landscape.

Another border crossing, Pennsylvania only containing a short stretch of 20. Now, peopled Ohio. Not as many farms, more buildings, houses, signs of population.

Interesting architecture of the governmental buildings of Painesville. But I just pass through, making my way west.

More peopled, but still country. Aroma of wood smoke from a chimney and a yellow caution sign:

> *duck and ducklings.*

Near dark I cruise through Cleveland. Vice-presidential candidate Jack Kemp speaking downtown. Extra police and more traffic than what is probably normal. And a poet goes through unnoticed. The poet/Buddhist d. a. levy's city.

> "Sometimes city
> when i walk at night
> i slip into your past or future
> and there is nothing
> except walking at night
> and silence"[*]

I drive into the night, stay in motel somewhere west of Cleveland, feeling a not wise use of the limited cash on hand.

[*] From the poem "CLEVELAND UNDERCOVERS" in d.a. levy collected poems by druid books, 1976.

Day 5

Breakfast at "Sterk's" on the west edge of Wakeman, Ohio, a small
midwest country crossroads town. Homemade peach preserves and
Amish cookbooks and cooking video for sale. The video, "Amanda's
Amish Kitchen" intrigued me. I live on the edge of an old order
Amish community and was surprised to see this video of Amish
cooking. Seemed a little too modern from what I know of the
Amish. Of course, the box doesn't say that Amanda is currently
Amish!

> walk after breakfast
> blue water tower, gray sky
> Wakeman, Ohio

Railroad used to pass through here but now all that remains are a
few grain buildings, a Depot Street and no sign of railroad tracks.

Three times a Wakeman police car drove by as I was walking
through town. Coincidence, or am I suspect because a stranger
walking through town, stopping now and then to write in a
notebook? It made me recall the slight paranoia in the old days
when walking through towns, pack on back, thumb out to passing
cars. "Oh no, a police car. Are they going to stop me?" They almost
never did, except in a few cities, never the small villages. This car
never stopped either and it may only have been my slight paranoia
from the old days. Then again, maybe not.

Billboard somewhere west of Wakeman:

> GET US OUT
> OF THE UNITED NATIONS
> The John Birch Society

Just east of Norwalk the brakes on the old car started getting soft.
Brake fluid was low so I filled it up and then within a few miles
again the softness. I drove slowly into Norwalk and came to a stop
in a Walmart parking lot. Crawling underneath, I discovered a rear
brake line had broken. Exactly the type of complication I was
hoping not to encounter! I was traveling with limited funds

so couldn't afford to have a mechanic work on the car. I pondered the problem for awhile and then came up with the idea of blocking off the lines to the rear brakes, continuing on with just front brakes (most of the braking is done with the front brakes.) So, I cut the broken line, had a nearby (how fortunate!) mechanic shop solder shut one of the lines I was able to take off the car, plugged the other one with a plastic bolt, then a test drive in the Walmart lot. Success! Back on the road again.

Heading toward Angola, Indiana and my first poetry reading of the journey, I thought about the brake problem and how I solved it. If I had resource to money, to dollars, if I wasn't making this trip on a bare bones budget, I could have had someone work on the car, fix it in a proper way and then move on down the highway. If I had dollars I wouldn't have been driving such a beat car in the first place. But I didn't have the money, have never had the money to just let others do the work for me. A long time ago an unconscious decision was made to pursue the path that I need to travel and to not make money a prime concern. If monetary success followed along, fine. If not, ok too. It hasn't yet, so I crawl under old beat cars trying to figure out how to get a few more miles down the road with the limited dollars on hand.

corn stalks turning brown
full harvest moon nearly here
road lies straight ahead

Because of the four-hour delay getting the car road worthy again, I felt rushed on the way to Angola. No time to stop, though various places called out to me. Toledo looked inviting. Tree-lined Maumee River with green parkways lining riverbanks. But there was a scheduled event coming up and time was of the essence. Maybe some future trip through the region I can explore Toledo and the Maumee. I'm just a stranger traveling through, sometimes hurriedly.

lull of car on road
where is it I'll sleep tonight
dead coon on shoulder

Angola, population of about 6,000, is the county seat of Steuben County. The Carnegie Public Library sponsored the reading and about 25 people turned out. This was the first poetry reading in town as far as anyone remembered. The audience ranged from a number of high school students to an 87-year-old black woman who shares the poetry of black poets to interested groups. She recited two Paul Dunbar poems that the audience loved. The library was very excited about the turnout and I encouraged them to build on this enthusiasm and to schedule regular poetry readings. It was especially exciting to have such a range of ages in attendance. People left afterwards with ideas already beginning to be generated on what to do next. Planting of seeds along the way.

Day 6

I've always felt there is no such thing as coincidence. All things happen for reasons.

In the morning as I was checking the oil level of the car just before leaving Angola, I started up a conversation with this guy walking by. He had a beard and long hair tied back in a ponytail. Seemed to be about fifty years old or so. Well, as we got talking, it turns out he is from Venice Center, not far from Auburn, NY and is on his way to San Francisco. Or at least, was on his way. His car blew a head gasket and he's stuck in Angola till he earns enough money to get it repaired. Also, I learned that he's a playwright and prose writer. We got into this great talk about traveling and writing. So here I was, about 600 miles from home, standing in a parking lot in Angola, Indiana talking about Japanese and German writers with a fellow writer and traveler who also lives in the Finger Lakes region of New York! And he says I should write on the side of the car:

KEN KESEY FURTHER REJECT!

So often life is like that. We make connections with others in circumstances that seem improbable at the least. How many people walked by I didn't say hello to? Why this particular person? Was there some sense of knowing that we shared common interests that led to that initial exchange? I pondered those questions as I drove down the road west out of Angola, feeling energized from our conversation.

The flatlands of northwestern Ohio have given way to the slightly rolling terrain of northeast Indiana. Rural farmland with signs pointing off to nearby lakes. Amish and Mennonite country. A horse and buggy pass by in opposite lane and a young woman with long skirt and bonnet rides a bicycle toward town.

South Bend. Red brick Route 20 for a few blocks, Colfax Ave. How many years before this relic of older days is paved over, modernized?

Moving on, going, going, going, not stopping this time around. Rolling Prairie and a long line of school busses come rolling down the road opposite me. The traveler passing through while everyone else goes about their daily routine.

Sand showing up along roadside cuts near Lake Michigan. Terrain keeps changing. This vast, wild, varied continent!

At Lake Michigan Dunes National Lakeshore visitor's center and one of the first trees I see is a sassafras. Oh, how the years evaporate, memories come floating in from a camping trip long ago! With my ex-wife near Harrisburg, PA in April. Finding sassafras trees, gathering roots and drinking cups and cups of tea while sitting around the campfire. Sassafras is reputed to help clean the blood but I've never read about aphrodisiacal properties. That night in the tent. . .

First hike while on journey. Dunes Ridge Trail. Old dunes anchored by oak and sassafras. Trail winds up and down tree covered sandy mounds.

> on sandy dunes trail
> two white puffballs, taste so good
> whitetail runs away

Eventually I make it to Lake Michigan, small Great Lakes waves lapping sandy shore. To the west - factory smokestacks of Gary. Northwest - skyline of Chicago. I think of Lew Welch's "Chicago Poem." This dune shored lake a brief respite before the onslaught of miles and miles of city/suburban madness.

Oil refineries. Smell of petroleum in the air. Industrial USA. Reminds me of 25 years ago, walking past Niagara Falls chemical plants on hitchhiking way from Buffalo to Niagara University to visit Michelle. How could anyone live near such a place?

Day 7

A pleasant day spent at my brother's-in-law house, suburban
Chicago. Took a day off from traveling for publishing work that
had to be done. An interlude from the road visiting relatives I rarely
see. Former Twin City residents transplanted to Chicago after years
in California. Fifteen year old daughter, with Doors, Joplin, Beatles,
Jefferson Airplane White Rabbit posters on the wall of her
bedroom. Another generation finding identification with the culture
of my youth.

Day 8

Getz on radio
blowing sax from Tanglewood
pre-dawn Chicago

I left 3:30 AM from suburban Chicago listening to jazz on the radio
and seeing very little other traffic. So much more enjoyable that my
entrance into the city with lines and lines of cars and miles and miles
of worn down streets not treating my old broken-leaf-spring Honda
very well.

Approaching Rockford, still dark, nearly full harvest moon showing
through breaks in clouds. Chicago, you're fading fast away!

Breakfast in Freeport. Four eggs, hash browns with melted cheese,
toast and coffee: $3.19.

A banner across one of the main streets:

Kiwanis Peanut Day — Friday

Red brick city hall with names carved along the top, just below the
roof - Dante, Shakespeare, Spencer, Chaucer, Homer, Uhland,
Rabelais, Emerson, Milton, Addison, Newton. . .

I stop at a Salvation Army store and buy a pair of lightweight
hiking boots and a wool sweater (might be cool out in the western
mountains) for $4.00. Reminds me of Kerouac's The Dharma
Bums, when Japhy Ryder (Gary Snyder) takes Ray Smith
(Kerouac) to a similar store to outfit him for the mountains.

I also learn here that Route 20 was locally known as the AYP road –
Atlantic, Yellowstone, Pacific.

Continuing on from Freeport the land becomes very picturesque.
I'm told that the road can be quite dangerous at times but didn't feel
any more unsafe than anywhere else. A controversy is brewing over
the possible changing of 20 into a four-lane highway. As it is now,
it is certainly one of the nicest stretches of Route 20 west of New

York State. I'd be very cautious about making any changes in that section of the road.

Galena, a quaint historic town near the Mississippi. Home of General Grant and eight other Civil War generals. The town has beautifully preserved its 19th century character. I took a walk down Main Street and then out over a graceful arched walking bridge that spans the Galena River. I felt like I didn't want to stay here too long though, too much of a market feel to it with just about all the buildings housing retail shops or restaurants.

brick buildings line street
storefronts displaying things, things
loose change in pocket

Stopped at Java Jeans for a coffee (spent some of that loose change) and a little journal writing time. The day is gray, breezy, cold - not one for sitting still outside. So I sit at a table sipping hot coffee, writing, watching people walk by the front window.

cold gray autumn day
yellow jacket buzzes by
flies into cafe

I crossed the Mississippi and entered Dubuque, Iowa. After bartering for a room in the Hotel Canfield I walked out to the great river and sat on its banks for 3/4 of an hour or so. Towboats pushed barges up and down river; ducks flew by in flocks, heading upstream in the darkening sky; small fish jumped out of the water. I sat at the great river's edge thinking how I was now on the western side looking east, looking toward home. I've crossed a border that has much significance. This river being a real boundary, not just an abstract line on a piece of paper. I've traveled beyond the mythic separator, the watery wavy line that is one of the great historic boundaries of this land.

After sitting on its bank awhile, I came to feel disappointed. This was not the Mississippi of my dreams, my visions. This body of water, still a significant crossing place, was a shadow of itself, a shadow of what I thought it to be. Here, on the doorstep of Iowa, the edge of Dubuque, this great river was not much more than an artificial reservoir, a dammed up body of water that had lost its flowing strength, its wild rushing ways. A diminished presence, controlled, harnessed, subjugated. A tiger in a zoo, a bird in a cage no longer able to fly free.

I turned from river, climbed dike to walk back to the hotel. When on top I noticed a red brick building: the Dubuque Star Brewing Co. My funds were limited, but I couldn't resist the tavern in the corner of the building. A large crowd drinking, talking, partying. Friday evening. Young and old in mostly casual dress.

I sit at the bar, order a pint of Pumpkin Ale. Dennis, the bartender, tells me a little of the history of the brewery. Started in 1898. The Pumpkin Ale is good, reminiscent of the pie, my favorite! I move to a table to sit, write a bit.

After awhile I get talking to Roger, a resident of Dubuque. He grew up here then left for about ten years, never thinking he would come back to live. The father of two, now seeing the Mississippi as an anchor, a foundation to rest upon, grow upon. I have another draft - Wild Boar Black Forest Wheat. A slight hint of cherries. Roger and I talk of spirituality, creativity, death while in the midst of this Friday night out-for-a-good-time crowd. We continue the talk outside on the front steps. I need to head back to the hotel, write the daily column, get some sleep and spend the day driving 320 miles across Iowa to Sioux City for a reading. I want to linger but there are promises to keep. As we shake hands he slips me a $20 bill to help out down the road, get me a little further toward my goal. Ah, the people one meets while on the road, the people one wants to get to know better! Sometime in the future, sometime when traveling this way again.

I walk down the dark night streets back to the Canfield. The landmark downtown hotel has been renovated but still retains its old charm. A fourth floor room with tub, porcelain sink, two cushioned chairs, end tables, table lamps. A comfortable, century-ago feeling. I imagine how many people have stayed in the hotel over the years. How many moving west like I am, driving route 20 across the plains and on out into the mountains, maybe even all the way to the Pacific?

Day 9

I headed out of Dubuque early, having the length of Iowa to drive. Route 20 climbs up out of the city past the modern chain motels, leaving behind the Mississippi valley, entering rich farm-country plains.

Breakfast in Dike, west of Waterloo, at the Barn Cafe. A sign in the entranceway:

> *OFFICIAL AGRICULTURAL SEMINAR*
> *HELD HERE DAILY*

Out front two small statues, a cow and her calf. Holstein. Farm country. Decorations on the walls inside - a hand washboard, eveners with a come-a-long hanging from one side, a buck saw behind me.

acres of dried corn
brown stalks, leaves sway in light breeze
blue water tower

Silos, barns, scattered old windmills, some missing blades, strong odor of freshly spread manure. East of Iowa Falls a number of round brick silos.

Iowa barns - gable-roofed, long slanted roofed, round, wooden, cement block, small, large and mostly white, alongside mostly white farmhouses.

Road straight, through cornfields, some bean fields. Silos in view almost continuously. Cows and cattle, quite a number of calves. Water towers, windmills. Rare sight in this relatively flat farmland country - wooded north/south ridge just west of Correctionville!

Sioux City. I walk in a park along the Missouri River, so much more a river than the Mississippi in Dubuque! The Missouri flows swiftly as it passes along the Iowa/Nebraska border. Just upstream from this park the Big Sioux River joins the Missouri. The power of water flowing!

A little bit of that empty feeling. I notice that it comes late in the day when I'm not sure where it is I'll put up for the night. Not a true traveler yet!

Sitting in the Anderson Dance Pavilion in a park by the river. A beautifully landscaped area with a covered pavilion for dancing and another dance circle out in the open. Flowerbeds, brick walkways, benches and the Missouri flowing just off to the west. A strong sense of peacefulness here.

Downtown's another story. The chief impression was that no planning or forethought had been put into the development of the area. There was nothing enticing me to park, get out of the car, walk around. What an opposite feeling from that of the river park!

Gave a reading at Pierce Street Coffeeworks. A musician from Wisconsin was performing afterwards. I didn't expect many people, but about 25 showed up, of varying ages. I read a series of poems about traveling and restlessness that the audience really to connected with. Barbie, about my age, said my reading inspired her to pursue her dream of taking off on her motorcycle next spring to wander around America. This time not on the back of the machine, but in front and alone! Donyell, an eight-year-old girl who came with her father, presented me with a picture she drew of me reading and two people listening. Todd, an ex-traveler, still different-roader, read a poem of his from 25 years ago. Another poet shared his poems for the first time in public. The expanding interest in creativity!

The value of sharing creative work. I read poems by other poets and sometimes my life is changed, added to, expanded. I share my work with an audience and sometimes someone's life is changed, added to, expanded. Art should do that, should change lives. It is a radical endeavor.

Another person told me that Sioux City is the jumping off point for the west. Many settlers came, stopped and then stayed here because of fear of what was ahead, a fear of going off into the wilderness, into the unknown. I head off to sleep, not with fear, but with anticipation for what tomorrow will hold as I venture into the northern Nebraska grasslands and sand hills.

Day 10

Left Sioux City late in the morning after a good breakfast talk with Mary, a woman I met at the reading who put me up for the night. She's publishing a small paper in Sioux City called the *Sow's Ear*. It's distributed free and contains probing bits of sarcasm, wit and satire. Her purpose is to shake up the city, try to get it moving in a more community-spirited way. She feels it is a company town in the worst of ways - a meat packing industry that has taken and taken and given very little to the community. Another person committed to place, working to make a change in the life of the home territory.

I crossed over the Missouri River, entered Nebraska expecting a continuation of the same type of terrain. Well, after a few miles I felt as if I was on Route 20 back in New York State! Dairy farms, cow pastures, hay fields and woodlots all set in rolling hills. The vast corn fields and flat land left behind on the eastern side of the river.

Entering Orchard, a teenage boy running in grassy area along side of road trying to herd a flock of sheep.

20 follows along the Elkhorn River, though most of the time the water is out of view. A small river, but the name conjures up a vision of Native Americans.

Beyond O'Neill corn disappears, cattle and hay predominate. Some of the hay, huge mounds stacked in the fields, appear like little brown hillocks.

A momentous happening near Valentine, about two thirds of the way across the state - I entered into the WEST! Farmland gives way to sandy soil. Trees pretty much disappear, grass covered hills slope away into the distance. Mile after mile of shifting shapes trailing off in every direction. This landscape totally different than anything I've seen so far. I felt as if this was the real turning point in the journey. The Mississippi and Missouri rivers were boundaries of a sort, but there wasn't that much of a difference on the other side. But here, where the land starts to turn sandy and hills begin to appear, there is a definite look and feel that is different than any landscape along the previous 1500 or so miles from Boston. This is where the west begins, on US 20 anyway.

> scattered cattle graze
> on fenced in grassy sand hills
> meadowlark takes flight

Intriguing, mystifying. The old Federal Writers' Project guidebook to Nebraska says these sand hills have been called everything from "the most fascinating region in the country" to "the most deserted and dullest." I agreed with the former, wanted to park the car, walk off into the distance and feel the energy that is part of this place. There really does seem to be some kind of force here. I can feel it as I drive by.

April, a clerk at a gas station in Valentine, told me that the railroad tracks that ran parallel to route 20 were just recently torn out. Old bed to be used as a long bike path that will eventually run from Chadron to Norfolk, over 300 miles. A fascinating environment to go bike riding through.

April also spoke about how things are changing here in other ways. The barriers between the sexes, or sex roles, are breaking down. Women out working, men staying home. Most couples living together, not married.

> torn up railroad tracks
> mountains of decaying ties
> stacked along highway

As the sun lowered in the western sky, hills started casting shadows to the east. I entered Chadron, a small college town, bartered once more, this time for a room at the Westerner Motel (seemed appropriate.) The owners, Larry and Janice, bought the motel after it had been deteriorating for a number of years. Larry tells me he went to New York City for a few days on a business trip. While there, he took in a Broadway show and says Janice will never forgive him for doing so without her.

Day 11

> breakfast by myself
> country music, waning moon
> trucks, cars hurry by

> heart wanders far away, east
> has frost come to our garden

Pine Ridge country. After breakfast I hike a small hill behind Chadron State College. So different than the environment back east, back home! Grass covered sandy soil with pine trees and soapweed - spear-like leaves and dried three-part seed pods, opened, seeds mostly gone.

This knoll, hill, ridge maybe 150 - 200 feet high, affords a great view in all directions. To the north, way in the distance, a glimpse of the Black Hills, a magical, mystical place I won't be visiting on this first journey west. Land of Black Elk, Lame Deer, other native people I recall reading about. Then to the west, the way of my travels, the first sight of buttes on the horizon. Yes, a totally new country, landscape.

> goldfinches, nuthatch
> call on pine ridge near Chadron
> close eyes, Wheeler Hill

Even here in the west, miles away from home, sand hills, soapweed and pine, the call of familiar birds, sounds I hear on hayfield, oak-beech-maple wooded fifty acres 1,500 miles away.

Beyond Chadron buttes dominate the landscape. I drive slowly, fascinated, taking in as much as one can while moving down the road.

Native American country. The most prominent butte in view, Crow Butte. In a battle, Crow fled to the top of the butte and then Sioux covered all the exits, waited patiently for days. The Crow knew they were trapped, but then they made an escape rope and the young men climbed down a cliff leaving the old ones behind. When the

38

Sioux, tired of waiting, finally attacked, all they found were the old men. The Sioux spared their lives and thereafter felt a special power in that place.

A few miles further on is Fort Robinson. Among other things, this is known as the place where Crazy Horse was killed. I stopped at the site of his death, a couple of reconstructed cabins, to pay my respect. Standing still in afternoon sun, no one going by, I tried imagining back then. Too many thoughts crowded in, too many western movie images to feel it in any real way. I bowed, moved on.

I took a long hike while at Fort Robinson State Park. The region was devastated by a forest fire in 1989. Charred trees, some still standing, give the area a very eerie look.

It was good to get out on my feet. I sat under a blowout in the cool shade of exposed sand and rock at mid-day, sunny hot, upper 70's.

> in shade of sandstone
> early fall like midsummer
> crickets, don't be fooled

While sitting at the blowout I discovered two different types of cactus only a few inches high but very numerous.

> cactus at my feet
> reaching to touch, needles sharp
> heartache long ago

For a few brief moments thoughts of the first person I fell in love with, all those many years ago. Ah, what if she were here now, what would that be like? Some memories, desires, sweet heartaches linger forever.

So good to take time to look at the small, the close at hand, instead of just moving on by, taking in the broad view as the small particulars pass unnoticed.

Back on 20, broad expanses of grass on a huge plateau west of Fort Robinson. Two dozen brown horses running along the crest of a rise, huge western blue sky behind. Ranch country, fenced in, private. The western ranges full of space, distance. Horses, cattle, sagebrush. A different landscape than anything I've experienced before.

Then, a few miles down the road, beyond Harrison, approaching the Wyoming border, the first far off glimpse of the mountains! I pull over, step out of car, take it all in. The highest and most distant peaks far off to the left. Tetons, maybe? Then, rows of mountains along the horizon till view is blocked by a rise of land north of where I stand.

I recalled a scene from my youth in Buffalo. Whenever we drove by the highest point of elevation in the area, Walden and Harlem, on our way to Thruway Plaza, I would look out of the back window at distant hills to the south. I gazed at them with a sense of longing, a sense of wonder, awe, mystery. They represented some far unknown territory that I vowed I would go to some day. Always the draw to distant hills, far away places.

Now, the western mountains on the distant horizon, again in a car, dreaming.

A sign proclaims:

> *WYOMING*
> *Like No Place on Earth*

Another memory flashes back as I pass the sign proclaiming the above. Nova Scotia. 1972. Terry and I hitchhiking through the province. Art, from Ann Arbor, gives us a ride, takes us up a dirt road to a bluff, 200 feet above the Bay of Fundy. We sit talking about Gestalt, Franz Perls, life changes, as the world's highest tides churn far down below. Driving back, away from the bluff, coming around a bend in the road, horses galloped in a field and I had a strong sense of being in Wyoming, no longer Nova Scotia. The sensation was but an instant, yet overwhelming in its intensity. 24 years later I finally make it in body.

I realize that in the last two days most of the big trucks passing by are cattle trucks.

Late afternoon, entering Lusk, a town of about 2,000. I try bartering books for a room and quickly find there are no rooms available. Tomorrow is opening day of deer and antelope season! It seemed there were a lot of vehicles around for a town this size. I ask at the local library if I can set up the computer, write my daily article and send it out E-mail. No problem, except they will be closing in 45 minutes. So I hurry, write fast, get it sent off just before they're ready to leave.

A draft at Sam's Saloon. About 25 people at the bar and around tables, mostly men. Some talking, others watching Monday night football. Relatively quiet for this many people. I sit alone, writing, reading. Realize I've been taking notice of women a bit today, more so than at any time during the trip. Also, thoughts floating back in time - Margaret, Terry, Sandy. The lonesome traveler!

The road is starting to seep into my being. It's at a point now where the moving itself is pleasurable, looked forward to, desired. Stay too long in one place, even a few hours, and I want to get back in car, go. Becoming a true traveler?

Clear night Wyoming sky. I drive out of Lusk a few miles, park on the side of the road, climb a fence, walk down a lane leading into dark, wide open ranch land. Lights of Lusk in the distance, universe of stars overhead.

Night sky, dark spaces. There's something magical about being out alone, away from people, surrounded by other than human, at night. I walk for about a half-hour, stopping occasionally, listening to night sounds. A slight breeze rustles something in the dark field, a truck's engine roars off into the distance down Route 20. Otherwise, quiet. I listen to my own breath, feel dry air enter my lungs. There are differences from the east beyond those that just meet the eye.

Sioux City seems so far away, time and distance. Only two days ago but like another world, a place I visited in some distant past.

Prairie View Campground just west of Lusk. Bartered a book for an empty campsite to lay down with my sleeping bag and tarp. I stretch out on bare ground, gaze up at waning moon, Orion, Big Dipper. October 1, sleeping out under the wide Wyoming night sky without a tent. I expected cold air, maybe snow, not this autumnal warmth.

Day 12

I slept off and on through the night, as is usual for a first night on the ground. Finally I got up, washed at a roadside rest area, bought a coffee to go at a nearby diner then hit the road at 4:30.

A whole different world than pre-dawn Chicago suburbs of a few days ago. No need for music on the radio, no desire for jazz. The music was in the sky, wide open night spaces, stars, moon, planets, vastness of 5,000' plateau Wyoming. This was heavenly! Orion and the moon shone off to the south, Big Dipper standing on its handle to the north and in eastern sky, bright Venus next to Leo the Lion, my daughter Cassandra's sign.

Headlights of a train approached off to the right. I stopped car, got out, stood under the vast wide Wyoming dome glittering above. The train's whistle blew a few times while passing, trailing off how many miles away across the vast prairie before losing steam? Clickety-clack, clickety-clack as the cars passed. Freight train, freight train passing by, under clear night Wyoming sky. Seven, eight minutes passing. I felt like a little kid, awed by the sound, speed, immensity of these huge freight cars rolling by. Then, just as I was ready to get in the car to continue down the road, another light in the distance from the opposite direction. This train speeding by much faster than the first. Old freight train Wyoming high up on the plateau.

Again, another memory from younger days in Buffalo. Jimmy and I hopping freight cars instead of going home for breakfast after receiving communion at morning mass. Then, a threatening voice yelling out from down the street, "Mikey, I'm going to tell your dad!" Aunt Eleanor did, I got yelled at, was forbidden to hang out with Jimmy. I continued to hop trains, just a little further away from home.

Douglas, population 5,076. North Platte River flowing quietly through. Cool, early morning, clear sky air. Breakfast of eggs and hash browns. Waitress asks if I want tabasco sauce. On edge of town an antelope grazes on grass at side of street, houses across the road. Smart place for an antelope to be on opening day of hunting season, edging into the city.

late moon, morning sky
Orion faded from view
first day of hunting

The Heritage Trail is about a 4 1/2 mile walkway along the North Platte, right in Douglas. So nice to have easy walking access to the river. Felt it would be good to get out for a little hike.

trout rise in river
eat early morning insects
after breakfast walk

walk along North Platte
long shadows in morning sun
yellow poplar leaves

Broken leaf springs on car giving me problems. Clamps not holding. Someone at the hardware store suggests I try muffler clamps. I buy a couple at the auto parts store, jack up the car, remove the tire, crawl underneath and clamp them on. This just might work!

I set up computer in the Converse County Library. One of the employees cautions me with, "Remember, it's frontier electricity here!" I spent an hour writing, no problem.

Back out on 20, an Atlas moving truck passes and I recall when an Allied truck driver picked Terry and I up on the "airline," a near hundred-mile stretch of remote road, Route 9, between Brewer and Calais, Maine. When we got to Calais the driver asked if we wanted to stay in "Allied Motel?" A great, thick bed of blankets in the empty trailer. No charge.

Glenrock. Kit Carson and thousands of others camped here. Names out of history class, old western TV shows.

standing by glen rock
settlers names carved in sandstone
white clouds drifting by

All life moves, moves, moves but the rocks seem to stand still. An illusion. A time scale much different than what we relate to. Settlers passing by 160 years ago in horse drawn wagons. I traveling through in an old beat car. The rocks sit, slowly move in their own way to someplace further on.

Dry, brown earth, but to the north of the road a line of trees, green and yellow leaves, bordering the North Platte.

When one gets into the swing of the road moving is what one does. Yet, there are places and people one wants to linger with for awhile. Casper is a city I could have lingered in for a few days.

I gave a poetry reading at The Daily Grind, a small coffeehouse near downtown. The Daily Grind is the place where the alternative culture happens in Casper. The owners scrape by financially, but feel it's important to have a place for poetry, music, creativity and good talk. A hangout, in the best sense of the word.

Greg, one of the owners of the Grind, is running for the Wyoming State House. 26 years old, involved with community and creativity. A welcoming, friendly person.

A nice turnout for the reading and an inspiring open reading. Charles Levendosky, former poet laureate of Wyoming, brought his poetry class along. He and some of his students read at the open reading. Charles, formerly from the east, knows another poet and good friend of mine, Stephen Lewandowski.

David, managing editor of the Casper Star-Tribune, offered to put me up when we spoke on the phone a few weeks earlier. So, after stopping in to see him at the newspaper offices, he gave me directions to his house and said his wife was expecting me. As soon as I entered I was made to feel as if I had been a friend of the family for years. Their three children were home too, ages 3 through 9. Seeing them made me miss my children back home even more. But we had a great time, a pleasant supper and then I had to head off for the reading.

When I returned, about 11:00 pm, David was on the telephone dealing with some urgent newspaper business (the life of a newspaper editor!) and his nine-year-old son was still downstairs. In between calls from the paper, the three of us sat at the dining room table talking about traveling, poetry, work. David told of how he first entered into the newspaper business (he simply needed a job, no romantic visions of journalism.) He also shared a few poems he had written years ago. Once, when he went out to answer the telephone, his son said, "I didn't know that's how dad started in the newspaper business and I didn't know he wrote poetry." Ah, what travelers can bring into the lives of others!

This experience made me think of *Knulp* by Hermann Hesse, written in 1915. A wonderful short book that nearly 20 years ago a friend read and knew it was about me, that I was Knulp, the wayward traveler bringing the experience of the road and the spirit of freedom into the lives of more settled people. Now, these many years later, still like Knulp, still the traveler bringing adventure into other lives.

I wanted so to linger in this city of friendly people. If it were the old hitchhiking days I certainly would have. But I was scheduled to give a reading in Cody and had over 200 Wyoming miles of Route 20 to cover.

Day 13

How can one cruise down Route 20 and not stop at Hell's Half Acre? I couldn't resist. Anyway, it was just about time for breakfast. So I ate at the little diner/store and then scrambled around for awhile just below the edge of hell. This half acre is more like 320 acres of a deep depression with strange rock formations caused by erosion. Sandstone and limestone spires, pinnacles, crevices of various colored hues. A strange landscape that I'd love to explore more of in the future, maybe even spend a night way down in the depths of hell.

Drove by some antelope in a field and burst out singing "Home on the Range." Just couldn't help myself.

Couldn't keep driving through this intriguing area without taking a few minutes to climb one of the small roadside buttes that dominate the landscape. I explored for a half hour, climbed up one of the sandstone buttes and just wandered around. What looks to be flat land from the road is really a landscape of miniature canyons and crevices. During this short walk I scared out a jackrabbit and a ground squirrel, heard but didn't see a raven and found a bleached white backbone of some long deceased animal. What a great half hour. I could explore this terrain for days and not get tired of it!

Route 20 swings north from Shoshoni and heads up through the Owl Creek Mountains and Wind River Canyon. Three tunnels have been cut through rock in the canyon and the Owl Creek Mountains rise precipitously on either side of the road. Suddenly, the mountains seen from a distance on the plateau in western Nebraska (they weren't the Tetons like I had thought) are rising almost straight up along the side of the road. Wind River Reservation. Arapaho and Shoshone land.

Passing through the north end of the canyon one comes out where Wind River ends, Bighorn begins. The bluffs to the north a very striking shade of red.

Stopped at Hot Springs State Park in Thermopolis to soak in the Bath House. A 19th century treaty between the federal government and the Arapaho and Shoshone stipulated that the waters from this mineral spring be made available to the public for free. The 104 degree water in the Bath House can be enjoyed for 20 minutes without charge, so I rented a swimsuit, 75¢, and had a great soak for the allotted time.

> mineral hot springs
> Arapaho, Shoshone
> my body thanks you

An employee at the Bath House told me they may start charging for use of the facilities. When I mentioned the treaty she said that the treaty was between the federal government and the natives. It's a state park now and they aren't bound by the treaty. It goes on and on and on.

> coming into view
> distant snow capped mountain peaks
> car engine races

Beyond Greybull a state rest area with a passive solar designed building! Exciting to see the state making use of the sun for warmth.

Cody, jumping off place for Yellowstone. I arrived in town late afternoon and bartered for a room at the Pawnee Hotel, the oldest in town, dating back to 1900. The owner, Jo Jean, gave me a copy of a poem she wrote in 1968 in praise of Wyoming. It seems as if everyone has written at least one poem in their life!

As I pulled into the parking lot of the Cody Coffee Co. the sun was setting beyond Rattlesnake Mountain, visible down the main street of Cody. Sun's rays streamed out from behind the mountain, a few cumulus clouds added depth to the darkening sky. I stood still, watched as the light faded, then stepped inside.

Paul and Beth, owners of the Cody Coffee Co., used to operate a coffee bar near Seattle. They featured music and poetry there but this was their first time doing so here in Cody. Another local poet also read and a singer/songwriter performed her original songs. A full evening of creativity. Nice to share the bill with a couple of talented local creative people.

1996 was Cody's centennial celebration. Dewey, who came to the reading, gave me a couple of issues of *The Cody Boobyprise, The Unofficial Unlicensed Irreverent Irresponsible Cody Centennial Newspaper* that he published this year. I think every community should have a similar publication to stir things up a bit.

Day 14

Learned that the road into Yellowstone is under construction and no one is allowed in after 10 am. So, I woke early and for breakfast had a great green chili skillet at Irma's. The restaurant is part of the hotel built by Buffalo Bill Cody just after the turn of the century. Antlers, stuffed animals, western paraphernalia adorn the walls. Certainly cowboy country.

Pat, the waitress, is originally from Michigan. A lot of the people I've spoken with are from back east. I understand why this area would lure easterners away. There's something irresistible about the open spaces and grandeur of the west that would appeal to individuals possessing a sense of freedom and independence. I've only come a little ways into the west and already can feel the lure, the draw that I could easily be taken in by. Would like to spend some extended time here in the future.

Teddy Roosevelt once called this road into Yellowstone the most scenic in America. For me it was both awe inspiring and horrendous. Awe inspiring scenery as the road follows the Shoshone River. Cliffs, towering mountains, snow capped peaks and the first rays of dawn lighting up the heights. Horrendous because of the road being all torn up for reconstruction. I thought the constant jolts, bumps and plunges were going to spell the end of the old Honda, destroy the last remaining remnants of leaf springs. I could picture the car being used as fill underneath the repaired roadway.

After getting beyond the road work I soon forgot about that annoyance (the car made it through OK.) I stopped at a pull-over spot and took a short walk down to the Yellowstone River. When I reached the river I immediately recalled pictures long ago in Field and Stream or Sports Afield showing fly fishermen on the Yellowstone. I think I walked down to that exact spot! It felt like I had been here before. Geese floated on the water, a blue heron winged by, some mergansers dove for food. What miles of rough road?

What is there that can be said about Yellowstone, America's first national park? Though I had never been here, I had an idea of what to expect from others who had, from pictures I'd seen, from the knowledge we acquire along the way about things of importance. I knew, yet I didn't know. There is no way of really knowing about Yellowstone until one is physically present.

The whirlwind tour. One can't do justice to Yellowstone in one day. I didn't want to be the car tourist zipping from one scenic spot to another, snapping pictures, looking without seeing then moving on. I chose not to drive to Old Faithful. Maybe the next visit. Instead I stopped at a few other popular spots and also made sure to get out of the car to travel on foot a bit.

At Artists' Point, an overlook of the Grand Canyon of Yellowstone, I left the crowd behind and walked off on a trail that led to Sublime Point. In five minutes walking I was removed from all the others and seemed to have the canyon rim to myself.

> fragrant conifers
> crowds left behind at roadside
> roar of waterfall

At this place I had an intriguing exchange with a raven standing on cliff edge about fifteen feet away. Whenever he called out, three hoarse croaks, I repeated the sequence back to him. He'd look at me, look away, cock his head sideways, call again. We repeated this numerous times. When I tried to get closer, moving ever so slowly, he flew off, calling out one more time as he left. I started to leave too, took a couple of steps, then heard a deep male voice but couldn't make out what it was saying. I looked up and down the trail but saw no one. I listened for some other sound, footsteps, more words. Only silence. Then some strong force drew me to canyon edge, to the depths.

> standing on cliff edge
> shadow lurking far below
> please come back to me

What would it be like to jump, soar down, for a brief moment airborne, then . . . I had to move back, sit down on a rock. Something uncomfortable going on here. Then raven appeared overhead, calling once more as he flew off across the gorge, out of sight.

There's power in landscape, forces that make certain places special, magical, mysterious. Raven's a trickster. I must go back there some day.

One could not help but create poetry while touring Yellowstone.

late morn October
bison lying in meadow
sunshine warms my face

bison munching grass
steamy breath rises upward
thermal springs breathe too

sulfuric acid
bubbling hot water springs
Japanese voices

Yellowstone River
rapids sing natural song
footsteps on wood stairs

dragon breathing smoke
roars from deep within a cave
bright sun, setting moon

Driving, I look up, see coyote walking along the side of a small gully. I stop, get out, take a few photos, then decide to hike up the side of the hill, leave coyote to himself. A few minutes later someone whistles from the road below then yells, "Coyote coming your way!" I turn around, see coyote ambling toward me a little ways down the slope. I wanted to stay still, see what coyote would do, but people watching from below were concerned so I walked away, circled round from where he came, returned to car. Coyote, another trickster.

Driving over Dunraven Pass, 8,859' then entering area where forest fires roared in 1988. A forest of charred trees, green coming up from below.

Wandered out into a deserted field where there was no great attraction. No bison, elk, coyote, thermal springs, gorge. No cars, people, cameras. A west sloping field in the late afternoon warm sun of an early October day. Near where field ended, woods began, I took off glasses, lay down in sun, closed eyes, relaxed. Alone. Quiet. I opened my eyes. Through tree branches - mountain peaks! A hawk soared overhead, too far away to identify. A cool breeze made me shiver. Then, from far away beyond woods, from somewhere out there in the vast Yellowstone distances, a bellowing, bugling call caught my ear. A sound I've never heard before, then silence. A few minutes later the call drifting through air once more. Bull elk's bugling for a mate reverberating in late afternoon western mountain autumn air.

Certain animal calls contain within them the whole essence of a region: loon, northern wilderness lakes; coyote, dry western regions; whippoorwill, southeastern states. Hearing elk once again, I smiled - I'm here in the mountains of the west. It's real and true and I've finally made it. Who hasn't longed to make it to the mountains, hear elk bellowing across the mountainous voids of space?

Then I thought of Sonny Rollins playing his saxophone on the George Washington Bridge during one of his hiatuses. What would that have sounded like to someone who couldn't see the source but heard it vibrating from somewhere out over the Hudson?

A little later I found myself at Mammoth Hot Springs visitor's center. Here, elk wander around the grounds, antlered bucks, mature females, young ones. Every once in awhile a bull elk would raise his head and give out with a call. Something was missing though. Here, surrounded by people, cars, buildings the call lost most of its magic. I felt let down, felt like I was at a zoo, no bars, but a zoo nonetheless. I was glad that I first heard elk's call while alone in the mountains.

I headed north out of the park to find lodgings for the night. On the way I caught sight of a few animals standing, climbing, scampering along the side of a cliff near the road. I thought maybe mountain goats. At the Blue Haven Motel in Gardiner, Montana I once again bartered books for a room. Bill, the owner, informed me they were female bighorn sheep that I saw, not mountain goats. How's an easterner to know these things!

This day in the park brought back recollections of my first visit to Acadia National Park in 1971, that first year hitchhiking on the road. Spruce and fir woods, rocky mountains, wild North Atlantic granite shore. A magical place that became a very important part of my life. I returned there many times after that first experience, lived there for a few years and still feel the need to go there often. That magic is here in Yellowstone, too. Something tells me I'll be back again before too long.

Day 15

The sun has not yet come up over the mountains to the east. I sit at Mammoth Hot Springs watching elk, feeling the crisp morning air. 26 elk are in view at one time. Some males bugle, attempt mounting females, chase other males away. The calls last from two to four seconds and are definitely higher pitched than what I would have thought. In the early morning light and not so crowded surroundings, the zoo-like feel of last evening is not quite as strong. These are still wild animals.

Mammoth Hot Springs. I wonder what it would have been like to have been one of the first explorers to come upon these bizarre fissures in this mountain wilderness? Steam rising everywhere, the strong smell of sulfur, grotesque landform and mineral deposit formations. Bizarre is certainly the right word for describing this scene. And I walk around reading informational signs, brochures that explain what it is I'm viewing, experiencing. What if I just came upon this scene unexpectedly? How would I have reacted? What would I have thought?

I lingered as long as I could in Yellowstone, but once again had to get moving on to another reading, this time in Ketchum, Idaho.

Driving toward the western exit I traveled through much burned over terrain with occasional patches of older, untouched by the flames, woods. Life forever continues to move forward, to grow.

Approaching the Norris Geyser Basin I couldn't help but think of the morning fog lying thick in Five Mile Creek valley way down below our property on Wheeler Hill. Steam hung over the woods, in clearings, rose up in the air from the numerous geysers in this part of the park. Geyser steam, valley fog, no difference.

Exiting the park west along the Madison River, traffic stopped for a herd of bison crossing the road. This too reminded me of back home, driving down the dirt road and having to stop while Carl moves his cows from one pasture to another.

So I left Yellowstone, traveled through a notch of Montana. Continental Divide at the Montana/Idaho border. Targhee Pass, 7072'. The Nez Perce, led by Chief Joseph, passed this way while trying to avoid capture by U.S. cavalry. Their homeland was to the west, they traveled east. My homeland is east, I'm traveling west, fleeing no one, a homeland to return to when journey over. Again, of what consequence is it that I make this trip?

A watershed divide. From now on, all the water I pass drains off into the Pacific, not east to the Atlantic. It seemed significant, but I couldn't really say why. I felt that I had been in the west ever since the Sandhills of Nebraska a few days ago. Even though that water drained into the Atlantic just like back in New York, the land was of the west. The continental divide marked the parting of the waters, but the difference between east and west was already marked a few hundred miles earlier.

Aspen at the peak of their color here. Everywhere bright yellow leaves. Not quite like the vibrant hardwood colored leaves back east, but still impressive.

Targhee National Forest in Idaho. For the first time in days, other than in Yellowstone, traveling through woodland. Mostly conifer plantations, but still, forest.

Off to the east this time, the Grand Tetons. Pointed high peaks in morning haze.

Idaho. I think of potatoes and lumber. Near Ashton, once again farmland. Plowed land, stacks of hay bales, an old barn leaning precariously toward the road.

Turning west from Idaho Falls, 20 travels through the Snake River plains. Much of this land is old lava bed. Three large buttes dominate the southern horizon while to the north and northwest lie ranges of mountains. Forested land has been left behind.

Pulled into Lost River rest stop and took a short walk. This area is where the first nuclear generated electricity was produced. 50 reactors have been built on the plains here, more than any other region in the world. On the walk I was excited to find my first piece of lava rock.

> magpie on dead tree
iridescent green feathers
dry Lost River bed

Entered Arco with a sign proclaiming:

> ARCO — First city in the world to be lit
> by atomic power

I was held up in Arco for awhile as the homecoming parade made its way through town. Horses, cars, trucks, fire engine, ambulance, old Cadillac convertible paraded the few blocks of Main Street Arco, which also happens to be Route 20. A clown came up and gave me a few pieces of candy. The Homecoming king and queen brought up the rear and I was the third vehicle behind following them through town. Almost felt like I was part of the parade.

Harvest season. Trucks rolling down the road loaded with Idaho potatoes.

Craters of the Moon National Monument. 83 square miles of lava covered ground formed 2,000 - 15,000 years ago. An eerie, otherworldly landscape that was pretty much avoided by pioneers, ranchers and miners. Looking at it, I can certainly understand why, but if time allowed I would love to explore it a bit more.

> abandoned old car
grown over with grass, sagebrush
ancient lava beds

27 mile drive off 20 to Ketchum for a reading tonight, workshop in the morning. Sun Valley, Sawtooth Mountains, moneyed vacationland! Didn't expect anything quite like this. Wasn't at all comfortable when I arrived. Too tourist dollars oriented with expensive shops, fancy restaurants, modern American resort business feel to it. Here I am with my old beat 83 Honda, short on dollars, still needing to raise about $90 to get me back home after

reaching the Pacific. If it wasn't for the reading I would not linger in a town like this.

The reading, at the Chapter 1 bookstore, went ok. Four people showed up, attentive and conversive. My expectations weren't high after getting here. Too much going on, too nice weather, not the right setting. Still, I enjoyed giving the reading and meeting those who came to listen.

Day 16

Early morning stroll through a sculpture garden on the grounds
where I stayed the night. The house and gardens sit next to the
Wood River, Sawtooth Mountains rising across the water. I walked
alone around the garden, taking in the metal artwork, river, rugged
mountains. There was an energy in this place that I felt but couldn't
identify. What a marvelous place to be on a sunny October
morning!

The juxtaposition of two sculptures caught my attention. One,
Festival Device for the Feast of St. Joseph, the other, untitled. The
festival piece: old machinery, iron wheel, saw blades, spring steering
wheel. The untitled piece: two layers of four white cubes each
separated by white poles, two horizontal, one vertical, all mounted
on a black base that had four designs on them that looked like the
circles of growth on cut tree stumps. These two pieces next to each
other made me dwell a bit on the changing ways of society. While
doing so, the rising sun suddenly illuminated the peaks of the
mountains across the river. What is there to say, what is there to
think? Some works of art are timeless.

Breakfast at the house and good talk with Joseph and Ellen, whose
house I stayed in, and Charles, visiting from Grand Rapids,
Michigan. Art, creativity, politics. Afterwards they headed out for a
morning hike in the mountains. I had to head off to conduct a
workshop at the Sun Valley Arts Center. The day was too nice,
sunny and above normal warmth, to sit inside for a workshop, but I
was committed. . .

Most others felt that way too. Still, a good workshop of writing
from the visual arts. Paintings from various galleries were displayed
at the center. We used those as starting points for our writing. A
haiku I wrote during the workshop:

> first sight of magpie
> lava fields stretch forever
> dark secrets untold

Sally, who works for the Sun Valley Arts Center, gave me a poem she had written about Route 20, "In State." Another person connecting with this old road.

The drive to Boise stretched through dry, brown, desert-like Idaho. Sagebrush and fenced in ranches for mile upon mile along with distant views of various mountain ranges. To the north of the road and west of Ketchum, huge clouds of smoke bellowed up from behind one of the mountains. A wild range fire I assumed. Forty miles later I could still see the smoke.

One of the major differences here as compared to the hills and valleys back home is that ability to see for miles and miles. Here the horizon is far, far away, unless there is a nearby mountain range. One gets used to distant focusing whereas in the Finger Lakes the view is usually of the next hill on the other side of the valley or the nearby woodlot. Space as opposed to containment.

I pulled into Boise at about 5:00. One of the first things one notices is the wonderful sight of trees everywhere! Boise, true to its name, is a city full of trees. After miles and miles of brown landscape the sight of so much greenery is a delight for the eyes.

Stopped at a downtown coffee bar for a couple of cups of brew and a bit of journal writing. A nice comfortable place with an eclectic mix of tables, chairs and couches. Back in the old hitchhiking days there weren't any places like this around. The greasy spoon or fast food joint the only options. They certainly had character but a place like this is a delight for weary bones.

While sitting with coffee I think about how I'm four days from the Pacific, four days from the end of the journey, Boston so distant from where I now sit. I want to be present as much as possible with the rest of the journey, not be thinking of what lies ahead, what's gone behind. Yet, thoughts come of themselves - don't resist, just flow along.

Made my way to the Log Cabin Literary Center for my reading. An Idaho Press Club dinner was in progress and they invited me to grab a plate and join in. I met someone who was originally from Buffalo and then was introduced to another person who used to live at Bluff Point on Keuka Lake, not too many miles from my home on Wheeler Hill. People were so friendly and talkative that I had a hard time getting around to eating my plateful of food! While sitting outside at dusk, numerous flocks of geese flew by, calling out as they passed above the Boise River. A nice sight and sound that connected me with home.

The Log Cabin Literary Center just opened this year and is doing a great job of presenting readings and workshops. The city has leased the building, an historic structure, to the center for 30 years at a dollar per year. The center needs to maintain the building, which is a big expense, but their membership is already beyond what they predicted for next year!

When the director of the center introduced me, he mentioned that this was the first reading scheduled because of initial contact with their web site!

I started the reading with this poem:

> How can one sleep
> when all night
> geese call
> while passing by

At my suggestion we scheduled an open reading to follow my reading. Four readers took part and for two of them it was a first time experience. This was also the first open reading to be held at the Log Cabin. They're planning to incorporate more of them since the initial one was so successful. A little more planting of poetry seeds.

Stayed the night with Gary and Diane at their house on a hill overlooking downtown Boise. A quiet place at the end of a dead-end street, lights of the city shining below. Reminded me of Robinson Jeffers' poem, "The Purse Seine."

Day 17

Again, wanting to linger a while longer than the schedule allows. A great morning on the deck overlooking Boise. Mocha, talk about local politics (Gary is running for Highway Commissioner,) the natural world (Diane is an editor of the Idaho Fish and Game magazine) and poetry. Quail running around in the yard and the Owyhee Mountains visible in the distance to the west. Gary brought out some old poems to share that he wrote during the "beat" period in 1959. Diane had never heard them before. I couldn't help but think of David and his son back in Casper. A little spark set off, old poems resurfacing.

Boise, a beautiful city full of friendly people, but once again having to move on down the road.

So I entered the final state of the journey, Oregon. Not more than 10 minutes later I was stopped by a county sheriff. I knew I wasn't speeding and couldn't think of any thing I may have done wrong. Well, he stopped me because I didn't have a sticker on my license plate. I tell him New York doesn't have stickers on them. Still, he wanted to check my registration and license. He returned a few minutes later after checking me out and told me he couldn't write me up for anything so he was just giving me a verbal warning. "A verbal warning for what? I haven't done anything wrong." He agrees but still says he had to warn me. And I have 458 more miles to drive in Oregon!

The next 130 miles I didn't see another police car but I couldn't get David Crosby's song, *Almost Cut My Hair* out of my mind. The long hair, the beat car.

Onions and sugar beets grown in eastern Oregon. Hay, too. For awhile anyway, then back to brown ranch land. Different than Idaho and Wyoming - here there are hills. The dry stretches of those states were either flat or dotted with buttes. The fascinating, changing landscape of the continent.

Now, green amidst brown hills.

rounded brown mountains
green banks of Malheur river
quench my hidden thirst

After leaving the Malheur valley the road climbs over two passes in
these unnamed-on-the-roadmap mountains: Drinkwater Pass, El.
4212' and Stinking Water Pass El. 4848'. Maybe these mountains
aren't mentioned on the map because they are relatively insignificant
compared to many of the other mountains in Oregon. Yet, I really
enjoyed the ride through the small canyons, over the passes, along
the crests. Once again, as has been the case for most of the way
since the Sandhills, distant mountains line the horizon.

Another sunny, hot day. How many has it been now? Hasn't rained
since I left Chicago. Not just sunny, but warm, too. The wool
sweater I bought way back in Freeport has yet to be worn.

Stopped at Burns and decided to put in for the night. Once again I
exchanged poetry for lodgings. Jim and Bunny operate Bontemps
Motel. An older motel (no phones in the rooms) with about a
dozen units spread around a courtyard. They've owned it for 12
years. A pleasant couple who gave me a bit of information about
the area.

I still had an hour or so before dark so I asked where I could maybe
get out for a little hike, as most of the land nearby was private. They
told me to go up 20 a few miles and then turn right on a paved
road to get to some public land. So I drove there, turned on a
gravel road that climbed up a hill and happened upon an old
abandoned radar site. About a couple dozen metal buildings now
used as walls for graffiti by the locals. Was weird to see this ghost
base out in the middle of nowhere. I later learned from Jim that the
place was set up shortly after W.W.II and then abandoned in the
mid-60's. Relic of the cold war era.

abandoned buildings
radar site on distant hill
three mule deer stand, stare

I then took a hike around the hilltop and discovered a rock outcrop with a terrific view to the west. I sat on the edge of one large rock and looked off toward the setting sun. A valley below me, another row of hills beyond that, both covered with juniper trees (weeds, Jim said later.) As the sun set behind the western hills I thought how there are so many marvelous solitary places to explore in the west. Lying below me, miles and miles of National Forest and very few people. The only human presence I could observe was the light of a car on a road miles away. Then a few coyotes barked and yapped somewhere down in the valley below. I thought of that police car stopping me soon after entering Oregon. The coyotes called out once again. I smiled to myself. Another brief moment of realization that I am certainly in the west.

Back at the motel office, Jim showed me pieces of obsidian that had been collected in the region. Chunks of green, red, black volcanic glass. He told me I should be able to find some at Glass Butte, which I'd be passing on Route 20.

Day 18

Filled up with gas before leaving Burns. I ask the attendant what the weather's like here in May. "Nothing's been normal for ten years, so I can't begin to tell you what it's like."

```
Wild Horse Corrals Road
```

```
Sage Hen Hill Road
```

Juniper and sagebrush country.

A feeling of lightness, contentedness, this morning. Buoyant.

A small waterhole along the road with about three dozen coots swimming in it. I suspect any standing water in this high desert country will have its gathering of waterfowl.

If any bird typifies the west it has to be magpie. I've seen them in populated areas and in desolate sagebrush wilderness. Always present, always noticeable.

A few crows fly by and I realize that I haven't seen the great congregations of crows here that I notice back east.

I had this feeling, or maybe understanding, that one of the main differences between the east and the west is earth, ground, dirt. In the west, at least pretty much ever since the Sandhills of Nebraska, the earth has always been visible. Even if there are plants growing, like sagebrush or juniper, they don't totally cover the ground. There is always exposed earth to be seen. In the east the feeling I get is of growth, plants, trees, greenery. A lushness that is foreign to the west I've been driving through. Oh, there's places here and there that might be considered green, but they are far and few in-between. The banks of a river are like that, but out beyond the banks it is again brown dirt, earth. Yet, it is not all the same, the land is varied and diverse, even in its brownness. I do wonder what it is like here in spring, in May, even if May is never normal anymore.

Drove down a side road near Glass Butte and collected obsidian from the ground. All black, no green or red treasures to take back.

The high desert. 11:00 am and it already must be near 80 degrees!

Far to the northwest a glimpse of snowcapped Mt. Hood, maybe 120 miles away. Once again, the vast western distances.

There is more litter along the side of the road here, west of Glass Butte, than I've seen anywhere in the previous 3,000 miles.

> ### Lizard Creek Road

Thought of stopping in Bend for the night but then decided to keep moving on to Sisters and the Cascades. Busy, touristy Bend, the mountains are calling.

Sitting at a picnic table at the Sisters Motor Lodge, waiting for the owners to return. A note on the office said they'd be back about 1:00. A nice place with literature in the office, flowers surrounding the deck, beautiful views of the snow-capped mountains: Three Sisters, Broken Top, Bachelor.

The owners returned, one of them walked up to me and I asked about bartering for a room. She agreed and we started walking toward the office. Suddenly she stopped and asked if I had a credit card. I told her I didn't. She awkwardly said she couldn't barter for a room then. I told her I could call a friend and she'd let me use her credit card. No, that wouldn't do, it had to be mine. So, the barter fell through and I went away feeling a little dejected. She wanted it for insurance I guess, security, just in case I wasn't trustworthy, would maybe walk away with some of the room's furnishings. I thought about Vachel Lindsay tramping through the Midwest exchanging poems for room and board. Was he ever asked for security? I drove away thinking this place was too fancy anyway.

So I sat on a bench in front of the Sisters Post Office having one of those moments of self doubt. Mid-afternoon, needing a place to put up for the night and not sure what to do. I guess the asking for a credit card affected me quite a bit. Was I just a wayward tramp? If one didn't possess a "piece of plastic" were they suspect, less trustworthy, to be looked down upon? How to certify the basic goodness inside? This occupied my mind for quite sometime as I sat on the bench. I finally came to the conclusion that if there was a problem, it wasn't my problem. Some folks are just less trusting than others, need to feel more secure, not willing to take as many risks. In no way did this reflect upon me, was not a judgment of who I was as a person. I was certainly no less a good human being because I didn't own a piece of plastic that guaranteed my financial solvency in the eyes of others. I remember once using one of those plastic cards, years ago, to scrape the ice off the windshield of the car.

In the hitchhiking days my backpack always drew the attention of passers-by and would lead to conversation. Here, sitting on the bench, no backpack in sight, how could anyone tell I was a traveler full of interesting adventures to talk about, someone worth putting up for the night? I hesitated approaching people, asking for lodgings. Ah, there is so much left to learn about being a true traveler. I have spent too many years away from the road!

I walked along the main street and stopped in a used bookstore to browse for a while. Didn't have money to buy anything, and of course, I did see a few books I would liked to have purchased. One of the down sides of just scraping by. Now, if I had plastic!

The owner of the bookstore suggested the Conklin Guest House, on the edge of town, as a possibility for lodgings. So, I drove out that way and almost didn't stop because it appeared too fancy, too nice of a place for this beat middle-aged, ex-hitchhiking traveler with not even enough cash on hand to make it back home. A big, white ranch house on the outskirts of the village with nicely landscaped surroundings, beautiful views of the mountains, a small pond and a feeling of contented luxury. But I pushed myself, pulled into the drive with the sagging, rusty Honda wagon, walked up to the porch, spoke with Marie (the owner, along with Frank, her husband) about bartering books for a room.

We so often make assumptions after viewing outer appearances, even though we know that is a shallow way of relating with the world. I have a beat car, long hair, beard and expect some people will relate to me in a certain way because of that outward appearance. Maybe the plastic-desiring motel owner did. And I see a nicely kept bed and breakfast ranch house and think there's no way the owners will accept me.

I like it when my assumptions are shot down, proven wrong. Frank and Marie were very willing to barter for a room. They gave me the "dorm," a little "cubbyhole," as Frank says. A double bed, three singles, small desk, rockers, chairs, closet, bath in the hall. A cubbyhole of pure comfort and coziness.

The guest house is surrounded by a sprawling meadow and has views of the snow-capped Three Sisters peaks. A beautiful, comfortable, nearly 100 year old ranch house that is just the perfect place to return to after a long hike in the Cascades.

After unpacking I took a hike up around Black Butte, an over 6,000' mountain in Deschutes National Forest. It was too late in the day to hike all the way to the summit so I wandered, in the near-80 degree heat, on some of the old logging roads lacing its sides.

> traffic far below
> dusty world left far behind
> soft breeze cools my back

It felt so good to again set out on foot instead of sitting behind the wheel of the car.

> fern fronds turned golden
> towering Ponderosa
> pine cones at my feet

> counting rings on stump
> two centuries on mountain
> burial headstone

All in all, I hiked about six miles around Black Butte feeling exhilarated and a bit drained. I drove back to the guest house, stood still for a few moments before entering, watched the fading light in the west beyond the mountains.

twilight's softened glow
pond water reflects mountains
tired body rests

After showering I sat downstairs in the sitting room with a glass of wine, cheese and crackers. How often I've found simple pleasure sitting down at night with a glass of wine. As I sat there alone, in pleasant, comfortable surroundings, I couldn't help but think about how this journey would soon be ending. Tomorrow night in Corvallis then the Pacific shore the following afternoon. A little sadness crept into my being. It is so hard to be totally present! Yet, I didn't fight these thoughts, this feeling of sadness. I thought them, felt them, then walked upstairs for a good night's sleep.

Day 19

Woke early and took a nice hot mug of coffee outside to the gazebo. A frosty, clear morning in the mountains.

> coffee steams from mug
> my breath too rises upward
> snow on mountain tops
>
> laughing quack of ducks
> ripples spread out over pond
> mountain peaks tremor

Breakfasted with a rock climbing couple from New York City. Seems some spectacular rock climbing spots are located in the Cascades. Then, as I started up the stairs to pack up, Frank said he wanted to speak with me before I go. I loaded the car then found Frank in the kitchen washing dishes.

"How'd you like to see the mountains from up in the air," he asked, "my plane is just across the road." So, we headed over to the airfield and then he took me up for an amazing experience I never dreamed I would have.

Before taking off, while prepping the aircraft, he recited to me "The Lavender Cowboy," the extent of his memorized poetry. Frank attributed it to Robert Service, saying it was his shortest poem, though I've not found any reference to it in Service's works. Whoever wrote it doesn't matter. The important point being that this was a lyric memorized, recited to another. This is how the tradition carries on, has carried on, will carry on, forever and ever.

What a totally different perspective to look down upon a landscape instead of looking up at it. Sitting in the Cessna as we propelled over and around the Three Sisters, Broken Top, Black Butte, I felt like an eagle or a hawk. Bank, dive, climb and all the while scenes of snowcaps, glaciers, mountain lakes, waterfalls, cinder cones, lava flows. And there, winding through the wooded landscape, the road I will soon be driving on again, heading west toward the Pacific, the end of the line!

I recalled the rejection I felt at the first motel yesterday. I smiled a little, knowing I would never have been in this plane if I hadn't been turned down by the owner. Thank you!

We landed, said good-bye, and I drove off from Sisters, climbed up and over the crest of Route 20 through the Cascades.

> wanting to linger
> highway calls to ocean shore
> come spring I'll be back

What a different world the western side of the mountains! Suddenly the dry ponderosa pine forest gives way to douglas fir, brushy undergrowth and a real sense of green. I felt as though I was back in the lush eastern landscape of home.

Passed a sign proclaiming "Sawyer's Ice Cave" so I had to check it out. I turned around, parked and walked along what seemed to be a path into the woods (there were no signs other than the one on the road.) In a short distance I came across a huge opening in the ground. I scrambled down in and wandered back as far as I could, maybe 100' or so. No ice, but about a 30 degree drop in temperature from the outside.

I couldn't help but think how just a little while earlier I had been soaring high above the mountains like an eagle or hawk and now I was scrunched up against dirt and rock in cool dampness inside the earth like a woodchuck or mole. Then soon in the car and back on the road again, just like a human!

A pleasure to walk on moss covered ground, to smell fir, feel dampness. Reminds me of Acadia!

The road follows along a small river. I stop, again get out on foot, walk along the bank, sit down.

> leaves drift down from trees
> clear water carries them away
> how far will they go

From here, all water flows to the Pacific. I try not to think about how near I am to the edge of the continent, but those thoughts can't be helped.

> dried leaf on shoulder
> long journey nearly at end
> seeds sprout in spring warmth

A delightful ride through the western side of the Cascades. Fir forests, water, curvy windy road, little traffic and a sense of the east. Flocks of crows and a field of orange pumpkins! So far from home, yet so much feeling like familiar country.

Stopped briefly in Albany to do laundry before continuing on to Corvallis and my last reading of the journey. At the laundromat I totaled up my cash and figured how much I still needed to get me back home after reaching the coast. Definitely need a good turnout for the reading.

At the laundromat I gave Jennifer a call. We had contacted each other through the internet after I did a search for haibun on the web. Her name came up and when I checked her page found a piece of haibun she had written. She gave me directions to her house in Corvallis and told me to meet her there after she got out of work. Jennifer helped to set up the reading that I was giving, sponsored by the Willamette Literary Guild.

> connecting through space
> computer technology
> soft smile, warm, friendly

At Jennifer's a brew and pleasant talk with her and her roommates. Then a walk back downtown to Grassroots Books, where the reading was to be held.

Corvallis, a college town on the banks of the Willamette River. (Jennifer tells me it is the largest north flowing river in the country.) Bookstores, coffeeshops and a lot of young people. About equal distance from the Pacific and the Cascades. A pleasant feeling place.

The reading was held upstairs at the bookstore. About 15 people showed up. Very attentive and appreciative. Michael, who works at the Book Bin, another bookstore in town, read a poem about Lew Welch after I had referred to him in a piece I had read. Linda, a teacher at a local Community College, shared some work from an anthology the school had published. Afterwards a group of us went out to "Squirrel's," a local gathering place, for food and talk. So often the gathering together, the going out after a reading, is so fine and enjoyable. Good talk after the sharing of creativity. There are great, friendly, creative people everywhere.

Michael put in an extra plea for donations, saying they didn't want to see me get stranded in Chicago on the way back home! The group was generous and I felt much better about my prospects of being able to afford the trip back. There would be no room for splurging, but I should be able to eat simply, buy gas and pay tolls without having to worry too much. Ah, even near the end of the journey, still not feeling like a true traveler!

Jennifer's roommate Jill showed up and the three of us lingered at "Squirrel's" after the others left. Good conversation that went below the surface, scratched at the doors of some deeper wellspring.

We walked back home through late night Corvallis streets, continuing our conversation. After getting back, I decided to sleep out in the back yard. We spread out a ground cloth, I brought out my sleeping bag and then settled in for another night of sleep out in the open.

Day 20

My last night of the journey. I didn't sleep very well. It wasn't because of lying out on the ground in the damp, foggy Pacific air. Over 3000 miles and now the end of Route 20 was just another 65 miles to the west. What value sleep when there are roads still to travel, a vast western shore to approach?

I awoke in the Corvallis back yard to a dark and foggy morning. Well, not quite morning, or at least not quite light yet. I dressed and then took a little walk through the pre-dawn foggy streets. Such a joy to have the coolness of morning mist hanging in the air! Yes, the ocean is not far away.

Today I felt like lingering awhile. Today I had the luxury to do so. The end of the road was only a little more than an hour away.

I visited with a few of the people I met yesterday at Jennifer's house and at the reading. I stopped to visit Michael at the bookstore where he worked. We talked awhile about writing, Oriental poetry, creativity. I read a few poems out loud in an aisle of the store and he gave me a book of 17th and 18th century Japanese fiction to take along.

I sat at a table outside the Grassroots Bookstore on 3rd Street with a coffee and my journal. People walked by smiling, saying hi, shouting greetings to each other across the street. Couldn't help think of Market Street, the "arts block," people back home. I lingered and lingered, wrote and wrote, not wanting to leave, not wanting to depart Corvallis, not wanting to get to the end of the journey.

> fog in morning air
> beyond mountains, high desert
> heart full of people

While sitting, I thought about the final few miles ahead. I wanted to be with the journey till the end, not yet take time to reflect, not think of the 3100 miles behind me, the people, experiences, landscape. There was still an hour and a half to go. I was still on the journey and needed to be present for it, not have my mind somewhere on the road behind.

women walking by
eyes, body, mind enjoy sight
bird footprints on sand

It's not easy being present when so much has happened in these last 20 days.

I drove out of Corvallis as the fog was evaporating away. That seemed appropriate. Route 20 winds through wooded hills and small fields on its way to the Pacific. Conifer trees and deciduous trees whose leaves were turning color. Numerous high-piled log trucks headed east. I stood on a small bridge over the Yaquina River and every time one of the loaded trucks went by the bridge would bounce and shake. Numerous hills displayed signs of having been clear cut.

The fog was entirely gone now and the mid-afternoon sun was hot. I moved on, wanting to go slow, pulling over at pullouts to let the faster moving vehicles rush on by. I wanted time to slow down, the miles to somehow extend themselves. I was anxious and yet sad. Endings are so final. Somewhere down the road 20 would be no more.

Toledo, a few miles before Newport. Fog could be seen in the distance. I stopped at the grocery store, wandered around, bought a couple of supplies, wrote in the journal. Back in the car like so many other times.

I think there were vistas from which I could have seen the Pacific if it weren't for the heavy fog out over the water.

I reached the limits of Newport, followed the road toward a busy intersection. Routes 101 and 20. A busy gas station on the right, other businesses lining both roads. Somewhere beyond the buildings, somewhere out in the fog, the great western ocean!

This was it. U.S. Route 20 ending at a tourist town intersection. No signs proclaiming the end of the road. No special markers, nothing to indicate anything other than one more intersection in the great vast network of American highways.

I pulled into the gas station lot, parked the car near the last Route 20 sign high up on a pole, walked across the street, took a few obligatory photos. The journey ended, nearly 3,200 miles traversed over a thread connecting the two coasts of America. I recalled that first sign back in Boston hanging askew on a pole. Was it just twenty days ago? Was it really that many miles away?

I walked the few blocks down to the shore. The sound of waves on sand was constant, a roaring from out of the gray blanket, the ocean heard but not seen. On the sand I approached the sound, came into view, limited though it was, of the Pacific. The great western shore. The end of the continent. I breathed in salt air, felt the foggy dampness, touched the cold north Pacific water, stood still for a long while, staring out into the amorphous grayness, into the nothingness.

journey now over
vast continent at my back
ocean laps at feet